Beyond a Blast From the Past!

CHECK OUT ALL THESE

★ GOLD NUGGET GUIDES ★

★ *Rockin' with the Rules*
Understanding the Ten Commandments

★ *Beyond a Blast From the Past*
Discovering why God made you

★ *More than a Splatball Game*
Squaring off with the giants in your life

God Rocks!

Beyond a Blast
From the Past!

Discovering why
God made you

Standard
PUBLISHING
CINCINNATI, OHIO

Published by Standard Publishing, Cincinnati, Ohio. A division of Standex
International Corporation. Printed in Italy.

Written by Lise Caldwell. Art by Chelsea Road Productions, Inc. Project editor:
Robin Stanley. Art direction and design: Rule29. Cover design: Rule29.
Production: settingPace.

Scripture taken from the HOLY BIBLE, NEW INTERNATIONAL VERSION®. NIV®. Copyright © 1973, 1978, 1984
by International Bible Society. Used by permission of Zondervan. All rights reserved.

ISBN 0-7847-1355-3

09 08 07 06 05 04 03   9 8 7 6 5 4 3 2 1

CONTENTS

WELCOME TO ROCKY RIDGE . . .

. . . And Stone Church, where the local rocks come to praise God! Pastor Jasper, the minister there, is often considered to be the most sparkin' rock in town because he loves God's Word and he can preach it! This humble preacher even enjoys some cosmic hip-rock now and then!

Rocky Ridge is the home of Chip Livingstone. In many ways, Chip is just an average guy. He likes to play with his dog, Ruff, and tease his sister, Nuggie. But at a young age, Chip started a praise band with his friends called The God Rocks!

One of his friends, Splinter, is the smooth stone who plays bass in the band. Before he became a Christian, music was just a technical thing. Now he really digs writing and rehearsing songs that praise the Creator with Chip, Gem, and Carb.

Chip's mom and dad, Ruby and Cliff, work hard to teach their family about God's love. They also look out for Chip's friends and are The God Rocks! number one fans.

Mrs. Crag, the teacher at Rocky Ridge Academy, and Deacon Dug, Gem's dad, are always ready to help out where they can. Everyone at Stone Church is just one big family!

So come along and get to know The God Rocks! and their friends a little better. You'll have a rockin' good time!

AN OVERVIEW OF
A BLAST FROM THE PAST

Have mutant vegetables invaded the planet? Splinter sure thinks so when there's a mysterious explosion on the edge of town during The God Rocks! concert. All of Rocky Ridge is in a panic until Chip volunteers to take the band to explore the crash site. Will all those hours watching *Rocks in Space* finally pay off? When Gem discovers a mysterious yellow ring, Splinter is sure it must be an alien mutant vegetable mind-probe ring.

Chip's rock hound, Ruff, is the one who *really* solves the mystery. It isn't aliens at all—only a traveling soap salesrock named Buck. He's a space rock who has spent a long time searching for the meaning of his life. Floating alone in the galaxy, he is unaware that God created him and loves him.

With the help of Chip and his friends and Pastor Jasper, Buck hears the story of how God made the world. And he learns how special it is to be a part of God's creation, because God made *everybody* and *everything* with a purpose.

How can you have a *blast* with this book?
Look here and find out!

Crack open these pages and get ready for a rockin' good time, as Chip Livingstone and his friends learn that God created everybody and everything with a purpose.

How do we know what that purpose is? God tells us all about it in his Word, the Bible. When some people asked Jesus what God most wanted them to do, he answered, "Love the Lord your God with all your heart and with all your soul and with all your mind" (Matthew 22:37) and "Love your neighbor as yourself" (Matthew 22:39). But what does it *mean* to love God and love others?

Each chapter in this book tells a story about the God Rocks and their discovery of how amazing God is and how everything in his creation has a purpose. After each story you'll also find . . .

* Thinkin' It Through—questions to help you think about the main point of the story

* Buck Talks Change—Buck's thoughts about God's creation. As a universal traveling soap salesrock, he's seen a lot of it!

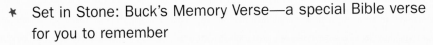

* Set in Stone: Buck's Memory Verse—a special Bible verse for you to remember

* Get Rockin'—great ideas for you to put God's Word into action, including some space for writing down your thoughts

If you want, you can read a little bit of each chapter every day so you have plenty of time to think about the story, answer the questions, learn the verse, and put God's Word into action. Or read a chapter all at once! Whatever you do, have a great time discovering why God made you!